ARCHIVE OF DESIRE

ARCHIVE OF DESIRE

A poem in four parts for C. P. Cavafy

Robin Coste Lewis

ALFRED A. KNOPF

NEW YORK

2025

A BORZOI BOOK
FIRST HARDCOVER EDITION
PUBLISHED BY ALFRED A. KNOPF 2025

Published by Alfred A. Knopf,
a division of Penguin Random House LLC,
1745 Broadway, New York, NY 10019.

Knopf, Borzoi Books, and the colophon are registered
trademarks of Penguin Random House LLC.

Library of Congress Cataloging-in-Publication Data
Names: Lewis, Robin Coste, author
Title: Archive of desire : a poem in four parts for C. P. Cavafy / Robin Coste Lewis.
Description: First hardcover edition. | New York : Alfred A. Knopf, 2025. |
"A Borzoi book"—Title page verso
Identifiers: LCCN 2025001213 (print) | LCCN 2025001214 (ebook) |
ISBN 9781524732608 (hardcover) | ISBN 9781524732615 (ebook)
Subjects: LCGFT: Poetry
Classification: LCC PS3612.E98 A89 2025 (print) | LCC PS3612.E98 (ebook) |
DDC 811/.6—dc23/eng/20250529
LC record available at https://lccn.loc.gov/2025001213
LC ebook record available at https://lccn.loc.gov/2025001214

penguinrandomhouse.com | aaknopf.com

Printed in Canada
1st Printing

The authorized representative in the EU for product safety and
compliance is Penguin Random House Ireland,
Morrison Chambers,
32 Nassau Street,
Dublin D02 YH68,
Ireland.
https://eu-contact.penguin.ie

in memoriam

MOHAMMED BAQIR 'ALWAN

for

DUNYA

You burn me.

—SAPPHO

CONTENTS

I.

HANDKERCHIEF

Handkerchiefs, ties, an old man
on the street selling loose
freshly roasted nuts

from a bright blue cart.
Is there anything
lovelier?

I know—now—
it is only a matter
of days (if I am lucky)

until I, too, stand somewhere hoping
another human will stop
and find what I'm offering interesting.

Blacksmiths—a bottle of black
ink, the address of your home
in Egypt: 10 Rue Lepsius—

the postage on the envelope
was only three halfpence,
a British king in profile, in dark

and bloody burgundy,
the alphabet purple,
on a typewritten letter

from Virginia
Woolf's husband, imploring
you—again—

to step forward
into the whiteness
of the page.

"Dear Mr. Cavafy,
The few translations of your poems
which we have seen . . ."

And then further down, in
the closing paragraph, he wrote:
"I hope very much

that you will consider this
favorably." Your letter back
to him—the quietest *No*—

is written by hand.
On another small sheet
of paper—

attached to a meticulously copied
poem, transcribed in cursive
and tucked away

into a private place within
your archive—you wrote, "This poem
need not be published. But it may continue

remaining here. It does not deserve
to be suppressed." By which you meant:
After I am dead, it may be read.

Another note
scratched quickly on a small pad—
in pencil—in the hospital—

just a year before
you died—when you
could no longer speak:

"Where have I placed you?
My tears are the only
testimony of my sincerity."

A photograph of your room—the silver
in the paper shines out from your bedpost.
How did you fit them—plus

all the twelve gods
and your desire, too—
into such a small bed?

An admission ticket—to the Lafayette
Gallery in Paris—in Alexandria—
written in French, then Arabic.

A circle with a larger circle
off to the left, then an oblong crescent
inside of that.

Some words scribbled
sideways. At the top, the letterhead says
The Hellenique Hospital

of Alexandria. And I think about you,
after so many words—*worlds*—
unable to speak at all

for the last
two years of your life—
how your voice

was always
drenched
in deep blue ink.

And how
often you
reminded us that

the only true
barbarians are the ones
raging in silence inside

of our own
minds—
and

they don't give a damn
whether we wait for them
or not.

Deviance
and *diaspora*
rhyme.

To be scattered—
desire luminous
and in tatters—

and still. Our cells
voracious without
the promise

of any fixed history—
all of our secret names—ignited
and awakened—hurling themselves

off the volcanic cliffs
overlooking a bay named Marathon.
As if names matter.

They mattered.
Like maps.
For how many millennia

exactly have our species
chosen not to kiss?
Land instead of ecstasy.

I want to be like that
town built at the top
of an island, fortified

by ancient sight,
the humble houses huddling
warmly together—

doors caressing
the endless
black rock.

(That town
embroidered in bright white
along the rim of a black crater

formed twenty-one thousand years
ago—the only remnant—
besides the sea—of a volcano

that first began
erupting—like me—three
million years ago.

That kind of town,
which—because of where
the sun rises, then sets—

can only ever be seen
from far away, for one hour—only—
very, very early in the morning).

I want you
to walk toward me
that way—

the way that someone
born in that town
boards the ferry

toward lush dark rock
with outstanding
blind faith

because he knows
(although his eyes
cannot see)

the black
bright path
home.

Red and rust tufts
of grass bending
in the wind.

As our ship takes off,
a surge of foam
that reminds me of you,

after you've come
for me, and I've come
for you, too.

Like the ribs
of that ancient ship,
which washed up

in a delicate harbor—
just the crossed beams—
and then was gone by morning.

The way the women
are made of stone—
our blood iron.

The way each
person looks just
like every other person

I have ever met—
anywhere—
on any continent.

The way
the locals built
their houses with their back

doors to the volcano—
their front doors
facing the sea.

And the colors of lava—
the endless shades
of blacks and grays,

the gentle folds
of millennia—
the reds, the reds,

and the billion-year-old
hard, hard pinks.
The way the sea says,

Your tears
mean absolutely nothing
to me. So

give them to me (You
could never be
a burden).

The abandoned terraced farms,
the thousands upon thousands
of black stones

someone hauled
up the mountain
and placed together

diligently, to form
an elegant, unself-
conscious wall.

The earth carved.
That man's
bare feet—

how I wished
to hold them after sex
in the middle of my chest

and kiss them
and tell him
how I found even

his ankles beautiful.
How I'd suddenly imagined
the two of us

sprawled out, our heads
at the opposite ends
of my bed, reading

aloud to each other. All
of this I saw when
his sandaled foot walked by

me
briefly
one day

as my brother
and I
toured the ruins.

Every day I watch
my brother stare out
into the sea.

Sometimes, I think
I prefer my barbarians
over all

other company. All
the ways we are imprisoned.
All the ways

I have imprisoned myself—
like the particular blue
of the Aegean Sea,

which no artist can paint
nor capture. I am
the seven thousand churches

and the relentless marble—the elegant
knots, the common rope—the ongoing
reminders that we all began in caves.

The earth,
the earth—so black,
so black.

Walking outside on a warm night
then turning to look back
into the room I've just left—its warm empty light.

The photograph
of my mother
as a young new bride,

which I carry with me
everywhere.
The navy-blue leather

cover of her passport.
And always
the curve of the earth

like the bone in her jaw—
geometrically perfect, yet
barely perceptible.

All the fallen
and broken
statues inside

my heart—all of
my broken Aphrodites.
Sometimes, I feel my dead

mother tickling me.
And there are other moments when
I can hear her

giggling, joining me
in a private observation
regarding my countrymen's absurdity.

The secret,
the private,
the unknown. A girl

on a dock blowing
kisses unabashedly
toward us as our ship pulls away—

this ship that
each person boards
for different reasons.

The eighteen-year-old
boy leaning against the rail—
pimples, gangly—bad haircut,

which he believes
makes him compelling. Virginal
awkward bottom

who reeks above all
else with the need to be
pummeled for hours.

Two children stand nearby
on the deck, also delighted—
in their own way—

with the sensations
their bodies feel from the force
of the wind—that irresistible

fear. The oldest girl tucks
her shirt into her skirt to keep her
blouse from blowing up

and exposing
her flat chest. The younger
sister—clueless—

doesn't yet know
the future will arrive
for her

carrying two breasts
of her own, two lighthouses
her body might choose

one day to ignite.
I love the wind. And thought
of your hands

taking everything
from me. Demanding
all.

I want you
to demand
everything.

I can't stop thinking
about the young men who slipped into
Cavafy's carriage in Alexandria

in the middle of the night.
Why do they feel
so familiar to me, kin

who have been dead in another country
for over a century? Maybe it's me—
it's probably me—who's standing

at the helm of this ship wanting to be
pummeled endlessly like the virginal boy
I've always been.

Evchristo.
It means *Thank you*
in Greek. I think. The Eucharist.

When did I grow
so afraid to speak
my body?

Lately, no matter
which country I am
in, I have begun to see

the horizon
differently. Was it ever
a straight line?

Do straight lines
actually exist?
Maybe

this is what it means, what
occurs, as you age:
the realization

that what you once believed
to be straight was always
arced, always bent.

This most essential sacred face
reveals Herself now
so quietly.

And the horizon says, Yes,
this, too, is a part
of my expression.

Don't be afraid.
I am always
turning.

And at first, I thought,
after I arrived, that
I would rush out

to see the World, to look
at everything. But then
I decided to get back into my bed

and look around
at the Worlds
inside me.

And to imagine what your world
and my world might do with—
and to—one another.

I look out, past the Acropolis,
at a boat so casually navigating
the rough sea.

Its sail is
your unfolded, opened
handkerchief.

And how I love
when the wind moves against the ocean
with liquid symmetry—

all the waves advancing
in perfect vertical lines—
like your desire—

no weapons, just
an army
of deep blue force.

Like this country,
the home of my grandparents,
I contain countless

uninhabited islands—
places so simple they are too complex
for human beings to sustain.

The islands just stand there,
uninhabited—like me—above the water
millennia after millennia.

I am no longer afraid.
I will never again allow myself
to be afraid to be loved. Or to love you.

Who am I to doubt the World's reasoning?
And how remarkable it feels—finally—
to be that broken filly

upon whom no one would ever bet, yet
one day—against all odds—breaks
into the outside lane—and comes in first.

The handkerchief
in your vest pocket
is a kite soaring

within my sky
that day at the races
when I crossed the finish line.

II.

"EROTIC-FUGITIVE-BLISS"

CAVAFY IN FRAGMENTS/AN ERASURE

My words clear the ground

Incapable of caution

I circle forward and backward, upon

A divan of ebony adorned

With eagles carved in coral.

Return to the Great Nothing

In order for her to recover her childhood body.

Deeply asleep alabaster halls

Fear of the commonplace

(How restless are the gods).

A spring hare on the path—

Here and gone.

Pleasure stands always

Right before us, a row of candles—

Golden and warm—all the days melting

But still lit. Roses at your head—jasmine

At my feet. I still don't want to turn around

(The king is careless with disaster.

He demands his stallions leap *faster, faster*).

Deep inside me sits an old man—handsome—

With a newspaper in front of him, pondering

The years—his vigor, his elegance, his zeal. See

The amount of joy he sacrificed. His own. The sea,

Its depths. His first step. A citizen

Within the city of ideas. He never wavered

From his duty (We even interrupt the work of the gods,

Their statues listen, well aware—

Trembling and relishing).

But he will not be misled

By the *serious,* the *great,* or the *unique.*

From this first step where I stand,

I will climb higher. And even

Though you stand

On your own first step, you ought to feel

Triumphant and happy. To have come

So far is no small

Matter—to have survived

So much is your greatest glory.

Honor to you, who, in your life, set out, just

And forthright. Generous when rich,

More generous when poor—and always

Telling the black, exquisite truth.

A high honor is indeed due

Because when you saw the end appear

You finally broke

Through.

ii.

Cavafy:

"For certain people
there arrives a day

when they are forced to say
the great *Yes*—or the great *No*.

It is obvious, immediately, who
has the *Yes* ready within them,

and by speaking it, they are able to pass
over into their integrity, conviction.

Those who refuse cannot conceive of *regret*.
If the question was asked

they would—again—
say *No*. Still that *No*

will weigh them down
for all their lives."

iii.

When a window opens, it will be
           without consolation.

I pace back and forth
           without pity—without shame.

What are we waiting for?
           Why—then—such inactivity?

Why come out today purple—studded
           with amethysts—rings with resplendent

Glittering emeralds—yet bored
           with eloquence?

May our worth come always
           to have its say.

What will we become
           without our nightmarish fantasies

Of the barbarians? We are
           their children.

We are the Goddess's words—
      Her bracelets, Her rings,

We are Her
      intense and infinite wanderings.

iv.

for Terra, Tommaso,
Haile, Cade, Jayanti,
Simone & Cal—with pride—
in celebration

In the prime of this life, child, hold the plain

Instructions on how to tend the body:

Fashion a wreath

Made of black marble

With your eyes half closed. If

They say *disaster,*

Well, let's hope so!

Mere child, O

Great ancestral palace,

The blood in your veins:

We should boast of it!

(No, we know better) Time is just

A waterfall tinted a pale pink

With the gods' dark wine.

Gather together within, proclaim it.

The day a splendid array of hyacinths—

Warm. See: Deeply

Asleep lies Youth. Restless

Little House-Gods—trembling, trying

To hide their bodies—

One little god falling

Upon the other. Now this

Happens, and then that.

And in a year or two, the same—

Systematic and random—

In the exact same ways. They know

The Georgian and Alexandrian calendars

Are thirteen days apart. So let us ask them, then:

What is the Truth? What can such a small word

Possibly mean? We must return

To our own inevitability.

May sickness never touch them. May you

Each live the deepest of lives.

For you have understood

History's real sound—and you

Are the footsteps of the senses.

v.

Ambrosial perfumes,
      pearly combs to groom
      our raven-black hair.

For a long time now
      I've been working on finally
      giving my body its hooves—

Not to touch the ground, but
      to race
      upon the water.

vi.

And I shall not
            fear my passions
            like a coward. I shall
            abandon my body

To its pleasure, to delight,
            to the most
            daring desire—
            without any fear.

Like the heart of a seafarer:
            Sunbeams, the sun,
            the sea within.
            The air, the apparitions

Of the night.
            Nostalgia
            for arriving. Affection
            for what must disappear.

And I love
            the liturgical presence
            of our past, the years
            walking

Slowly through the narrow woods,
the grand second, grander
than the first—
your stout sensuous mind

Wrapped so carefully
in green
silk
want:

The secret
sound
of approaching
events. Your zenith, at last,
in your path.

Go out now.
No longer brush aside
or fail to bow—
even later—
to the serious and sudden

Midnight hour
(with its exquisite music)
that your Fate
is giving you, finally,
now.

You

      whom the gods found
      always deserving,
      move
      with steadfast steps

Toward life's window,
      listen, and look
      with colorless
      gravity.

vii.

and do not rest
        assured in your life—

settled, mundane, and
        invisible, disembodied

(I'd rather look
        at things than speak

about them). The sea this morning,
        the sky: cloudless—radiant

violet shore. The picture
        of my young body

inaccessible but fragrant
        Once, I sailed

in purple beauty—
        then I harbored a beauty

even the Gods
        were ill-equipped to put away.

And then
  you appeared:

You. The word: indefinable history—
  Lamp. Lamp.

I imagine, now, that you enter
  this room, that you stand, as always, right

before me—the joy of our mortality
  that bright black within your eyes.

Come closer, Beauty.
  Closer. Lie here with me.

Let's leave
  the window open

Again. My horses, my chariots, my robe
  all discarded. My senses trilling

In their silent serenity. Your skill—
  your love, your sorrow, your tongue:

Your right-to-left countersong—
        Your cadence—every phrase.

Your words wanted to know
        where my wounds are—

My vulnerable wonder—
        that suit of armor

I tried every day
        to keep constrained—for your protection.

Every day, I could see the coast. We were almost there—
        sailing upon the vast openness

Of our home seas. Joy,
        anoint my life. Find and hold

the pleasure lines
        of my time.

Night within night—Memory inside a darker
        Destiny, please, all of you,

sit down here at the table—
        Body, remember.

viii.

The Ancient Sanctuary
of Your Hand. Opened.

> The paradise of Your Attention,
> an hour entirely in the Courtyard

of Your Mind. The brilliant word
presence or *host*.

> The Procession of Life passes through
> our strength: the Holy Cross of Now.

In every District
of Distinguished Departure

> Life offers to be found.
> Was it ever possible for us

to relinquish such Beauty?
That daily union

> between art and flesh?
> Immoral talk about *taste*?

Devote our attention
to what?

                                    To hot-air utterances, the awkward
                                    self-glorified "mine" and "thine"—

those cold utterly
disgraced words. Reason

                                    to the extreme. Shame
                                    compromises everything.

And the injustice done
to the Oracle—the private citizen—

                                    for she is most aware
                                    of what the outcome will be.

O simple, pure,
sensual pleasure—

                                    O Splendid Edifice,
                                    O Great Host of Honor,

O Exceptional Wantonness,
O Attitude, O Untarnished Body—

O Beauty of the Years, O Mysterious
Surrender to Love for the first time.

I am the complete possessor
of pleasure. If you ask for more,

here it is, in plain words: In every art,
in every discipline, in sublime glory,

with the Procession's sacred torch—
the flutes, the lights—deep down

desire only to become
a sort of servant—a plaything—

to the give-
and-take

of this
fugitive night.

ix.

and pray that your road
    will be the kind of summer morning

        that you can ease into—
           unseen—to learn,

then learn again. To arrive
    there, anchor

        on the isle. Wait
          for that voyage,

which you constantly refused
    to set out upon, to find you

        with its meticulous experience.
          (And) Now, you have—finally—come

to know what
    it really means

        not to demean it
           by parading it all around,

exposing it
    until

        it becomes
          a stranger.

III.

CAVAFY IN COMPTON/CLOSET ANTHEM: SELF-PORTRAIT AT SIXTEEN, 1979

A TRANSLATION OF KONSTANTIN KAVAFY'S "I WAS ASKING ABOUT THE QUALITY"

I came out
of the office

where I had been
hired in another shitty, low-paying job

(My weekly pay was nothing more
than fifty dollars a week, most from tips).

With my waitress shift over, I came out
at seven and walked slowly. I fell out

into the street, handsome, but compelling.
It felt as if I had finally reached the full potential

of my own beauty (I'd turned
sixteen the previous month).

I kept wandering all around
the newly cemented streets,

the quiet and old black alleys, past
the cemetery leading to our home.

But then, as I'd paused in front of a clothing store
where some skirts were on sale

(polyester, cheap), I saw this face
inside—a girl—whose eyes urged me

to come inside. So, I entered—
pretending I was looking

for embroidered handkerchiefs.
I was asking about the quality—

of her handkerchiefs—how much
they cost—in a whispery voice breaking open

with desire—and accordingly came her
shop-girl answers—rote, memorized—but beneath her

words, her eyes kept ablaze: *Yes.*
Mine, too, were a psalm of consent.

We kept talking about the handkerchiefs,
but all the while our one and only goal was this:

to brush each other's hands—quickly—
over the handkerchiefs—to lean

our faces and lips
nearer to each other, as if

by accident. We moved quickly,
cautiously, yet deliberately—

in case her grandfather—sitting in
the back—were to suspect something.

IV.

"SHE HELD A DOVE WHOSE TAIL SURVIVES"

SELF-PORTRAIT AS THE ACROPOLIS

I want to be the marbled owl—the sacred bird—sleepless and with remarkable eyesight—that steady bird, which nests in the cracks of rock surrounding the sanctuary of the Goddess. Ancient neighborhoods I fly over at night—wing by wing—each city built upon—dependent upon—the silence of an older city buried beneath it. Is there even such a thing as land? Fragmentation is our anthem. Sun-dried bricks covered with packed earth form a brief wall above a paved mosaic floor. That would be my soul—if it could have a name. Small sacrifices to the underworld. The surprise of an abandoned underground well still gurgling. Funerary vessels. Terra-cotta covered with figurines of animals and birds. A kind of heart given to another to store cool water. My opened palm filled with bone pins, bone needles. A glass perfume bottle that somehow survived. I am red. Eros pulls me by the hand. More birds. Who is the sacrifice, my body or my mind? Small terra-cotta altars. The bones of a piglet. Dark figures on a light background. The Sanctuary of the Nymph. A baby's rattle shaped like a hare. Our love was so beautiful, every member of our family came up to bathe in the spring together the night before our wedding. My heart a spindle whorl, a fine clay weight, still spinning—faster and faster—within the abandoned sanctuary. My altar. My ever-flowing sacred spring. My door in. My gate out. God of Healing. God of Health. His wife and all his children. My black marble face inlaid with glass eyes. All the faces of the statues are melting. Magic sphere. Your spear tipped with magic—Protectress. All your nymphs stand, shoulder to shoulder, holding hands. Myrtle wreaths carved into a wall surrounding our names. All this happily lost so that in the future—now—they can be regained. Clay shards.

Iron blades. Fragments of gods. And the most efficacious gift of all: not to take history seriously. Each of us broken, each of us emanating an earlier glory. A procession of winged selves parading constantly throughout our cells—regardless of the red-dark harbor. Treasure box in the sanctuary inscribed with languages we do not need to know to understand. Our silence suspicious of anyone who believes they know where or when history began (It has yet to begin). Bronze axes, chisels, hammers, files. A mirror. Time claims all else. Countless warriors and charioteers. I see children and women running. A silver coin depicting a wheel. Daughter of God. Daughter of the Sea—born wearing a full suit of armor. Protectress of the City. Two lions maul a bull. A lioness mangles a young calf. I stand before you holding a pomegranate. My cape is woven with the small slender bodies of hundreds of baby-blue snakes, its fringe composed of all their minuscule heads—undulating and hissing. The Earth and Sky still like to make love. They still give birth to giants. A fruit, a flower, a wreath, or a bird—usually a dove. A bracelet in the shape of a snake on Her left arm. Tamer of horses. Winged Sphinx. The soft pink moonlight. And the little girls—all the brown little girls—whose bodies we buried in the Great Pit, which we dug by hand, hurriedly—for protection—the moment we looked to the horizon—the second we saw them coming.

V.

EPILOGUE

Love him and let him love you.
Do you think anything else
under heaven really matters?

—JAMES BALDWIN

I think the first time I ever fell in love was in second grade. Her name was Bridget. She was poorer than we were. I don't know how I knew this, but I would steal random coins out of my mother's pocketbook every morning so that Bridget could have lunch money. Maybe that is how I knew that we had more money than her family: there were actual quarters and pennies and dimes in the bottom of my mother's purse that went unaccounted for.

I've always loved women. I think it was inevitable, even cellular. Women had breasts and perfect hips, with those loaded, pregnant faces that held everything but confessed nothing. Besides the obvious aesthetic math, I was raised by the most gorgeous women who have ever walked the earth. Their very footsteps dazzled me. Their handsewn frocks. Their holy rage. Their eyebrows, their stockings hanging to dry in the bathroom near the red rubber douche. That secret world. Their rhinestone-studded pocketbooks and their mother-of-pearl pocketknives, the latter hidden inside the former—like their own interior weapons. The way not standing together was never an option. As many grandmothers, aunts, and female cousins as I had, they were all several versions of the same dynamic energy. Fire.

Feminine. And a profoundly deep ocean of what we now call *love,* but that word could never capture the infinity behind their eyes. The men in my family felt it and knew it, too. I grew up in a matriarchal culture dominated by a patriarchal society. We all knew how to play our roles, but we never believed they were anything other than that: roles.

So, it was never odd to me: Bridget. Why should it be? Other girls had crushes on very cute but very stupid boys. Why should I not fall in love with the smartest person in Mrs. Larson's class? I wanted to talk. And to skip. And to play. Perhaps that is all I have ever wanted next to me: a hot mind with a high propensity for pleasure.

Because I was one of the youngest of a large tribe of first cousins, I often read or played indoors (even then, books were more interesting to me than human company) when all the women of my family were together. It was there that I would hear things I wasn't supposed to hear. And this is where I still land: the women in my family were more intelligent than anyone around, including the strange white men on our brand-new black-and-white thirteen-inch television. They were also well-read, my mother and aunts especially. All their dark laughter seemed to hold every secret about the world, even while strutting out the door in pencil skirts and pumps to go and hear Nancy Wilson. Their complex beauty landed this hook in my throat—which, thankfully, has never dislodged.

So, I grew up enamored. And still I like to sit anywhere in the world and watch women go by, in silence. Many have decided to pretend to be just as boring as men, as a tool of allurement, in order to have children or company. I think men pretend, too, for these very same reasons. For aren't men all profoundly more interesting than our world allows? I grieve for the ways patriarchy strips boys of their childhood. The few times I have fallen for a man, it is usually because he has a beautiful boy still inside him, a boy who is smart and loves to play. Or maybe none of this has anything to do with the sham of gender. Maybe I just like intelligence and pleasure.

But why do I feel a need to explain? I owe no one any explanation about my experience of desire, except to say, as with most ancient religions, Desire is a God for me. And when desire and love meet inside my body simultaneously, as Rita Dove says, the sensation is "massive, inconvenient, undeniable."

And there is also History—always interrupting. Rupturing. So, it is important for me to remember that, when I was a child, women had to have their husband's written permission to apply for a credit card. Women could not get an abortion. I remember hearing women talk about the ways they were trying to terminate a pregnancy. Often. With liquor, with hard labor. Everyone likes to believe they were planned. I don't want to break anyone's heart, but most of us were accidents—and that might be the best thing about our births: how our parents had to rally to play their roles, to pretend that they enjoyed the eternal trap that love had set for them.

I remember my parents, thank god, not giving one turd for most gender roles ascribed to my sister and me. (Maybe it was because they were already exhausted by the gender roles assigned to them— "father" and "mother" or "husband" and "wife.") Like everything else shoved down our throats at the time, without much discussion, until we started our periods, my sister and I were mostly free to roam genderless. My father constantly put tools in our hands. We were always out in the garage helping him under the hood of his tan Maverick. *This is the starter. This spark plug is old.* It was nothing for him to say to one of us, "Go climb on the roof and straighten the antenna." We loved to take turns sitting on the buffer while he polished our wooden floors. Soldering guns, the monkey wrench, tape measures, spackling. We knew it all, as did our brothers. (I still love the sound wet cement makes when it's being readied by a bricklayer.) My father let me drive when I was three, sitting in his lap in our big Ford, his hands and mine on the giant steering wheel, as we glided down the empty freeway every Saturday morning to visit my grandmother, his mother-in-law, whom he secretly called Egg Head. And unlike many parents during this time, my mother and father refused to make my sister or me wear dresses or skirts. We wore pants, defiantly (even though, high femme that I was, I loved frilly dresses more, which made my sister roll her eyes).

And so, I guess it should not have come as any surprise to me when my father asked me one afternoon, affectionately and nonchalantly, "So, Baby, you a bulldagger?" When he saw the surprise on my face, he laughed. I wasn't shocked because of what he was asking. I was shocked because it was one of those hundreds of piercing times when I realized that my parents actually knew me better than I knew myself.

And I laughed because he imbibed a word that was traditionally vulgar with such affection. I knew then, as I have always known, that I was lucky. I was deeply loved. "Y'all co'tin'?" he asked then—by which he meant were my first girlfriend and I courting. I cracked up in his face, as only a child can do: delighted in my ignorance. "Dad, nobody courts anymore!" I said, feeling smart. My voice held a tone, the tone of the freshly assimilated clueless child enamored with the shine of a new century. He looked at me for what I was: a fool. Then he said that pregnant Black English word, which is only one syllable, but is sung in such a delicious, dismissive way that it contains whole philosophies: "Sheeeeeeeeeeeit!" *Shit,* but with the emphasis of centuries.

He was trying to tell me that sure, someone might love you, but love alone isn't the goal, because there is a difference between strong love and flimsy love. And courting could help ensure someone loved me strongly. He meant, Baby, if a person isn't willing to take the time to get to know you, or to let you get to know them, then they aren't worth your time to begin with. Was there a tinge of sadness or tragedy in his voice, too—sadness for the inevitable decades of romantic pain he saw rolling out before my life? It would take a series of failed relationships for me to understand precisely what *shit* meant.

My new girlfriend and I were maybe not courting, but we were inseparable. Michael Jackson's first solo album, *Off the Wall,* produced by Quincy Jones himself, had just landed. Imagine, two teenage Black girls, first-generation Great Migration descendants, falling madly and purely in love, driving around Los Angeles on her brother's motorcycle, me holding on to her from the back, living our lives completely off the wall, not stopping until we had enough. We would ditch school and drive down to Mexico for the day. We would ditch school and go to the beach and read poetry out loud to each other. The Los Angeles Unified School District (I will say this every chance I get) was deeply abysmal—racist, classist, xenophobic, plus underfunded and parochial. Indoctrination or babysitting passing for education.

We'd seen enough to know we could learn more on our own. So, she and I lied about our ages and took philosophy classes at El Camino College nearby—where we were happy, because there our teachers took our minds seriously. One of my professors, in a class called Death and Dying, smoked cigarettes throughout his lectures. I shaved off all my hair. My mother lost control and slapped me across the face when I walked in the door. Something in me smiled inside. Then outside. She was in shock. Then she cried. Then she apologized. Somewhere, in the middle of all this, a group of us, all Black queer teens in the late 1970s and early 1980s, left our suburban South Bay neighborhoods to go and see something called *The Rocky Horror Picture Show.* We also snuck out and drove across town again to see *Lianna,* John Sayles's early masterpiece—which showed us a world we could not possibly imagine. The Pride March was not a parade, it was protest, and only three blocks long then. We went and walked and stood proud—all of us teenagers.

Some of us found each other in Ms. Paddington's class in high school, before we took the proficiency test and dropped out. Ms. Pad taught the debate class, which was one of the best things about my high school. She kept her classroom open at lunchtime, and all the freaks, of which I was proudly one, hung out there. It was by far the most exciting place to be on campus. Ms. Pad didn't dumb anything down for us. She exposed us to every book she had, talking and laughing. Only now—now that I am a teacher, too—do I understand that she knew exactly what she was giving, providing. Besides Ms. Paddington's lunchtime conversation, and besides my white dyke middle school gym teacher, who realized I was weird and a reader and so handed me a copy of Lorraine Hansberry's *To Be Young, Gifted and Black,* neither I nor any of my classmates had ever been given a book by any Black author or any author of color to read in more than twelve years of education in the Los Angeles Basin. And so, it goes without saying that I had never seen any work by a queer writer, or read about queer characters, either.

I wish I could take my mind out and put it inside yours. I wish you could feel what it was like to drive around Los Angeles, to go to any city in the U.S., and find all the women's bookstores, all the Black bookstores, all the independent bookstores—take your pick! There were no bookstore chains feeding you only the middle-class bestseller list. None. There were bookstore owners and there were book lovers. On one of these trips, when I was sixteen and with my new girlfriend, we drove across town to Westwood, near UCLA, to go to our favorite women's bookstore, Sisterhood Bookstore. It was here—among the

"Sisterhood Is Powerful!" buttons, and the volumes of *Our Bodies, Ourselves* greeting us at the front door, as well as *The Joy of Lesbian Sex* (which made me blush hard), and Audre Lorde's *Zami*—that I found a volume by the remarkable Greek poet Constantine Cavafy.

There was before Cavafy, and there was after him. He was a window, a bright blue door, an open sea. He was a whole countryless country. I know many who cherish Cavafy's writing. But in addition to his aesthetic genius, this turn-of-the-century Greek poet, born and raised in Egypt, was a god for Black, Brown, Red, Yellow, and all of that mixed together, for baby Queers at a time when many were being kicked out of the house, beaten by their own families, and some positively disowned. It was Cavafy whom we read by flashlight under the sheets, or aloud to each other in a park or at the beach—in awe. We were elegant in his lines. Hell, there were lines. And his writing showed us that one could approach the classical world, which had been forced down our throats in our stupid classrooms as proof of white superiority. Of course, we all knew this to be a gross lie. He allowed us to reclaim the ancient world as a site not of indoctrination but of historical fascination. Because of Cavafy, the world became clearer, ours.

I think it was Whoopi Goldberg who once said that homosexuality is as old as air. And I think it was Freud who said that heterosexuality is the actual anomaly. I really don't give a damn. Now that I am an old broad, all I can say is: Gender is stupid. Let's set it aside and never pick it up again except to play with it for the toy that it is. What's more important to me are the worlds certain artists were able to create for us, worlds that did not exist before they began to think and write and create. And so, the true gift of Konstantin Kavafy, first and foremost, is his genius, his aesthetic, his craft. And all this he grounded within his courageous imagination via an elegant obsession with desire, particularly for beautiful men.

I don't know of any person of my generation, and certainly not any queer person my age, who doesn't stop in silence when the name Cavafy is mentioned. For many people who suffered isolation and abuse due to the complex and shame-filled web we call *gender,* Cavafy's poems saved their lives. Our lives. And his writing exalted our fugitive beauty. Or as the great poet Mahmoud Darwish once wrote, "For every rhyme a tent is pitched."

ACKNOWLEDGMENTS

In 2021, the artistic director of the Onassis Foundation, Afroditi Pana-
giotakou, commissioned the composer and producer Paola Prestini to
curate a multimedia festival in New York City, honoring the life and
work of Constantine Cavafy. For his 160th birthday, the foundation,
whose international headquarters is in Athens, Greece, proposed to
offer the world a two-week-long festival—for the love of poetry, and
Cavafy. Thankfully for us, they chose Prestini, and New York City.

I was moved when Prestini reached out to me to ask if I would
be interested in co-creating a multimedia collaborative performance
with composer, pianist, and sound artist Vijay Iyer, master cellist
Jeffrey Zeigler, and artist Julie Mehretu. I leapt. No one had said the
name Cavafy to me since I was a teenage girl trying to find my way
into my body. Prestini's idea to bring the four of us together resulted
in a collaboration and a production that will remain one of the most
profound encounters of my life.

To aid us in our research, the Onassis Foundation graciously
invited us all to Athens, where we could actually see and engage with
Cavafy's archive, which the foundation houses and protects meticu-
lously at the library of their international headquarters. Two thou-
sand of Cavafy's personal items, including his handwritten folios, his
letters, his belongings, photographs, notecards, and 966 books from
his personal library, are all there. The foundation has also digitized
Cavafy's entire archive in order to make it available to the public at
https://www.onassis.org/initiatives/cavafy-archive.

On the first day, Marianna Christofi, the Onassis Foundation's archive manager, and their staff had prepared a roomful of personal materials for us to look at. The tables were covered with Cavafy's papers and handwriting: letters he had written to publishers, to friends; notes to his brother; a list of shirts he needed for travel; sketches; his mother's passport; and one picture I found especially compelling, a photograph of his room in Egypt, with his bed—which he evoked so often as a site of lovemaking—buried under a pile of books.

For two weeks, we marveled. Cavafy never lived in Athens—he lived in Egypt—but he was born into the vast Greek Diaspora, and his writing exudes the tone of the historically diasporic. All of us had similar stories—water and migration and nation and war and colonialism and slavery on every continent—as well as the slippery sleight of hand called "borders." Each of us carried several of our own deeply problematic, mostly reprehensible countries within us. We didn't need to articulate our shared awareness of how our very bodies destroy the ideal that home could ever be a nation, or even a place.

I remember the first thing Julie Mehretu said on the day she arrived and walked into the room to join us. Always to the point, she demanded gleefully: "Where are the love letters?!" We all laughed, because where are Cavafy's love letters indeed? Because of Prestini and the Onassis Foundation, we were holding them in our hands.

We were stunned to be privy to all of this, in Athens itself, where thousands of years of history, including the grand history of homosexual love, is everywhere, sipping tea, right at your elbow, reverberating. I thought a great deal about Diaspora on this trip—how it is more verb than noun. I thought, most of all, that the word *diaspora,* whose meaning implies "to be scattered," for me actually means "to be found." We are constantly finding each other again—perhaps not in the same bodies, nor during the same century or millennium, but we recognize and remember each other continually. In Athens, almost halfway around the world, with Turkey just next door, contemplating the seas made legendary by Homer—and thinking, too, about all the objects, statues, columns, and temples that had been stolen from Greece, especially by European countries during the nineteenth century (particularly the U.K., France, and Spain), in some neurotic attempt to claim an origin that was never theirs to name—I was once again reminded of how blackness is also a verb, a home: the wine-dark sea.

So it isn't an understatement to say that the Onassis Foundation is on a rigorous mission of cultural recovery. At a time when we keep murdering our own aesthetic histories, making ourselves mapless, it was inspiring to see that they had just completed a project to install lights all around the Acropolis so that the entire city can view one of humanity's most revered ancient structures. And I thought, *Isn't it always the citizen who does the work of the nation?*

I was reminded of this especially on one of our final days in Athens. Iyer was departing a few days earlier than the rest of us. We were on our way downstairs to see him off in his taxi when Prestini casually asked the Onassis staff if they would allow us all, but Iyer especially, to see Maria Callas's piano. Our eyes threw words at each other. *Maria Callas's piano? Where? In this building?!* And so, after days of sitting with Cavafy's writing and papers, and yes, his handkerchiefs—all of it saturated with desire—we climbed down a flight or two and entered another salon, and there it was. La Divina herself. Her instrument. Her hands. Then Prestini asked if Iyer could play the piano. First Iyer just stood there, the room silent. He lifted the cover and began to tickle a few keys, so gently. Then he sat down. Most people don't know that Iyer used to be geeky physicist. But I think of him as a library. There is so much dancing inside his mind. He said, "I mean, Strayhorn," and began to play "Lush Life"—for Cavafy, for Callas, for the endless black sea of love. Like the men that Cavafy loved, Iyer was leaving sooner than we wished. His suitcase stood nearby. Departure. And so when he began to play perhaps the most celebrated but misunderstood closet anthem in American music, Strayhorn, who began this song when he was just a teenager, became one of our ship's companions, too: "I used to visit all the very gay places, the come-what-may places. . . ." Iyer left then, suitcase in hand, rushing to catch a plane. We all stood there, in awe. Callas, too.

Working with Jeffrey Zeigler—I don't have words. The cello, they say, is closest to the human voice. I had been listening to Zeigler for years, during his tenure with the Kronos Quartet, but also his remarkable work before and after. When we rehearse, I often have to sit down or, overcome, move my chair a little farther away from him, because whatever it is that artists do, that nameless, timeless thing that saves us every day, he does.

If there is anything of interest in this book, it is because I was trying to write what would please Cavafy and Greece itself, but also because I was trying to reach for something worthy of Zeigler's, Iyer's, and Mehretu's company.

Prestini also commissioned Laurie Anderson, Nick Cave, Helga Davis, Evi Kalogiropoulou, Julianne Moore, and Rufus Wainwright for the festival, too, just to name a few. It was an honor to engage in this work together. And finally, the festival included an academic conference on Cavafy, organized by the scholar and translator Stathis Gourgouris. For one whole week in the spring of 2023, thanks to the Onassis Foundation and Prestini, New York City was immersed in all things Cavafy.

For me, as an American Black queer, to imagine, to accompany, or even to allow myself to fantasize about becoming a queer Egyptian Greek diasporic male poet living in Alexandria at the turn of the last century was one of the headiest gifts anyone has ever given me. I imagined riding in Cavafy's carriage as he cruised Alexandrian men at night, inviting them into our coach as we roamed the streets— looking, looking, until early morning, making love here and there. Sometimes I just watched, sometimes I imagined myself as Cavafy, and sometimes I imagined myself as the man for whom Cavafy's carriage stopped. And I stepped in.

Was I making love to Cavafy's poetry, or were his poems making love to me? Night after night, our intimacy was folded into the papers—the letters—within his archive as I attempted to cast a net over all the intersecting colored and ancient centuries. Indeed, the painting and film Mehretu created for our performance was just this: a prolonged and deliciously queer visual seduction in the abstract— mark-making that enacted upon the audience the sensation of a glance, the quick touch of a hand, the eyes that ask, *Please, may we?*

For two years I walked with Cavafy, side by side, my arm inside his, discussing language and love. I think we both agreed that, at their best, language and love are the same thing. We would both dress in the starched linen suits he loved (for Cavafy's archive confesses a sartorial need for fine clothes, even when he was broke). I loved to adjust my tie in the reflection of shopwindows, smooth my mustache, and point out to him a man I found attractive, wondering about his taste. But it was most delicious to make myself a stranger to him, a man reclining on that tiny bed with him, and then to try to write from that perspective: the perspective of invisible but profound intimacy. The intimacy of the shunned, the outcast—how it makes desire sing when given full rein. Or sometimes, it was even more beautiful to imagine myself as his brother, how there are things, when we are older, that only a sibling can understand. And I was honored, as his brother, to listen to the insights about our families and histories, which Cavafy would whisper to me, as we sailed, again, back toward our ancestors' country. As it turned out, I positively adored being a gay man. I could finally say—even feel—things that I had never allowed myself to feel.

E V C H A R I S T O :

Thank you to the scholars and translators who have engaged with Cavafy's work for the better part of a century. Though I made my own English interpretations of Cavafy's works in order to create an erasure for this book, vast gratitude is due to the translators of Cavafy's poems, whose work accompanied me on this journey: Rae Dalven, Daniel Mendelsohn, Edmund Keeley and Philip Sherrard, Evangelos Sachperoglou, Avi Sharon. Most especially I wish to thank Stathis Gourgouris, the brilliant scholar and translator who was with us, courtesy of the Onassis Foundation, in both Athens and New York. When we questioned a particular translation, which rendered a word Cavafy used as the English word "deviance," Stathis was available to offer a more nuanced translation that mirrored the aesthetic of our project and that gave me the title of the second section of *Archive:* "erotic-fugitive-bliss."

Archive of Desire, the multimedia performance and live sound recording EP produced by VIA for the Arts, whose text differs in some particulars from the text in this volume, was commissioned by the Onassis Foundation and curated by Paola Prestini with creative producer Ras Dia. It was created and performed with Vijay Iyer, Julie Mehretu, and Jeffrey Zeigler, with additional music by Alexis Zoumbas; filmmaker Trevor Tweeten; lighting and projection designer Hao Bai; lighting and projection assistant Bryson Ezell; with sound designer Garth

MacAleavey, and additional photography and video by Tom Powel Imaging.

This performance project appeared at the following venues: National Sawdust Theater, World Premiere, Cavafy Festival, directed by Charlotte Brathwaite, 2023; the Palazzo Grassi in Venice, Italy, as a part of Julie Mehretu's exhibition *Ensemble* during the Venice Biennale of 2024; and the Broad Museum, Los Angeles, October 2024. (Further production and performance details can be found on the EP.)

I was honored that the Onassis Foundation decided to use the title of this long poem, *Archive of Desire,* to name their entire Cavafy Festival.

"Cavafy in Compton," first featured on the Academy of American Poets' *Poem-a-Day,* is a very loose translation of Cavafy's poem "He Was Asking About the Quality." It is dedicated to my dear friends Felicia, Kipper, Kevin, Oscar, and Robert Adan Williams, and to all my colleagues at the Shanti Project—especially Ed Wolf, Rafael Diaz, George Simmons, Erika Huggins, Nadia Babella, Sylvia Muniz, Melissa Villanueva, Dora Vintero, Irma Castro, and my dear friend Danza—with whom I worked at the height of the AIDS epidemic, and in memory of all the beloved friends, lovers, family members, and clients whom we lost. This poem is also dedicated to my colleagues and dear friends Ted and Baron. May we never forget that we lost the majority of our generation in a pandemic—and yet people still barely blink at that gaping absence.

The final poem, "'She Held a Dove Whose Tail Survives': Self-Portrait as the Acropolis," is dedicated to Brenda Shaughnessy, Julie Mehretu, and Paola Prestini.

On the book's epigraph from Sappho: thank you, Anne Carson, for these words from *If Not, Winter.*

Thank you to the Onassis Foundation, in Greece and New York, especially artistic director Afroditi Panagiotakou, as well as executive director Anthony S. Papadimitriou, and Dimitris Theodoropoulos, president of the board. Thank you to Onassis USA, especially senior adviser Karen Brooks Hopkins and festival producer Rachel

Katwan of Pomegranate Arts, and their respective staffs. Thank you to the Onassis Foundation Board of Directors: Dennis M. Houston, Florian Marxer, Stefanos P. Tamvakis, Michael-Spyros Sotirhos, Simon Critchley, Paul Holdengräber, Nikolaos Karamouzis, Panayotis Touliatos, Mary Karagianni-Michalopoulou, Eleni Panagiotarea, Konstantinos Bikas, and Peggy Antonakou. Warm and profound gratitude to Marianna Christofi, Onassis Archive manager, and Project Coordinators Angeliki Mousiou, Eleanna Semitelou, and Christina Kostoglou. Finally, thank you as well to Demetres Drivas, Alexandros Roukoutakis, Christos Sarris, Elisavet Pantazi, Christina Kosmoglou, Vasso Vasilatou, Katerina Tamvaki, Nefeli Tsartaklea-Kasselaki, Vasilis Bibas, Sylvia Kouveli, Giorgos Athanasiou, Margarita Grammatikou, Georgia Leontara, Constantinos Chaidalis, Jillian Viglaki, Theodoros Koveos, and Smaragda Dogani.

Thank you, also, to Pomegranate Arts, ONX Studio, Cause Lab, and Blake Zidell & Associates.

Thank you to the University of California at San Diego for awarding me the inaugural Sherley Anne Williams Writing Residency, where I edited this book, with gratitude to the Department of Literature's Sara E. Johnson, Brandon Som, Angela Booker, and Anna Joy Springer. Thank you to the Archive of New Poetry at the Geisel Library, especially the archivists. Thank you also to my colleagues at the University of Southern California's English Department and Dornsife College of Letters, Arts and Sciences, especially Rebecca Lemon, Dana Johnson, Janalynn Bliss, Flora Ruiz, Natalie Hunter, Lisa Itagaki, April Miller, and Tinna Flores.

Thank you to all the staff at Palazzo Grassi and the Teatrino di PG. Thank you, too, to the Broad Museum, especially Ed Patuto.

Thank you to the remarkable staff at Marian Goodman Gallery: Rose Lord, Gloria Vanni Calvello Mantegna, and especially Marian Goodman and Emily-Jane Kirwan, for your enduring support and intellectual and aesthetic community.

To the entire staff and crew at National Sawdust: Cori Aguilera Matos, Alexander Barnes, Kim Chan, Ana De Archuleta, Eve O'Donnell, Lynne Procope, and LeeAnn Rossi. Thank you as well to Brian Schuh, and to our director of sound and tech design, Garth MacAleavey.

Thank you to my publisher, Alfred A. Knopf, and everyone who supports me there, including Zuleima Ugalde, Ellen Feldman, Soonyoung Kwon, and my beloved editor, Deborah Garrison. Wylie Agency, thank you for the profound den of protection, most especially my agent, Jin Auh.

Finally, to my friends and family, who stay aboard this ship with me.

A NOTE ABOUT THE AUTHOR

Robin Coste Lewis won the National Book Award for *Voyage of the Sable Venus,* her first collection of poetry. The book was also a finalist for the Hurston/Wright Legacy Award and the Los Angeles Times Book Award, and it was named one of the best books of the year by *The New Yorker* and *The New York Times. Literary Hub* named it one of the best books of the last twenty years. Her second book, *To the Realization of Perfect Helplessness,* was the winner of the PEN/Voelcker Award for Poetry and the NAACP Image Award for Outstanding Literary Work in Poetry. She is also the coauthor, with Kevin Young, of *Robert Rauschenberg: Thirty-Four Illustrations for Dante's Inferno.* The former poet laureate of Los Angeles, Lewis holds a PhD in poetry and visual studies from the University of Southern California, an MFA in poetry from New York University, an MTS in Sanskrit and comparative religious literature from the Divinity School at Harvard University, and a BA in post-colonial literature and creative writing from Hampshire College. Her work has appeared in various journals, including *The New Yorker, The New York Times, The Paris Review, Transition,* and *The Massachusetts Review.* She is currently a professor of poetry and poetics at USC.

A NOTE ON THE TYPE

The text of this book was set in a typeface called Times New Roman, designed by Stanley Morison for *The Times* (London), and introduced by that newspaper in 1932. Among typographers and designers of the twentieth century, Morison was a strong forming influence, as typographical adviser to the Monotype Corporation of London, as a director of two distinguished English publishing houses, and as a writer of sensibility, erudition, and keen practical sense.

In 1930 Morison wrote: "Type design moves at the pace of the most conservative reader. The good type-designer therefore realizes that, for a new font to be successful, it has to be so good that only very few recognize its novelty. If readers do not notice the consummate reticence and rare discipline of a new type, it is probably a good letter." It is now generally recognized that in the creation of Times Roman, Morison successfully met the qualifications of his theoretical doctrine.

Composed by North Market Street Graphics,
Lancaster, Pennsylvania

Designed by Soonyoung Kwon